604

Anthony Quinn 604

Breakfast *in the* Rainforest

For Jonah: As you follow the trails into the jungle

Acknowledgments

The staffs of the Uganda Wildlife Authority and the Uganda Wildlife Education Center have been most helpful assisting me in my ongoing work in their country. I wish to thank the current and past directors of the Uganda Wildlife Authority, Robbie Robinson, Arthur Mugisha, and Moses Mapesa, and their field staff Lily Ajarova, Patrick Atimnedi, Gladys Kalema, Chris Oryema, Silver Mbonigaba, and Peter Moeller. At the Uganda Wildlife Education Center, I am grateful to Andrew Seguya, David Hyeroba, Alex Droma, Wilhem Moeller, Mukasa, Opeo, Grace, Barbara, and Jimmy. The kind staff of the Travellers Rest Hotel in Kisoro have been watching over gorilla trekkers for more than fifty years, and I thank them for their hospitality.

Dr. Richard Wrangham, Farley Mowat, and Greg Cummings have given me excellent field and scientific guidance throughout this project.

I am grateful for the support and encouragement of Irmelin DiCaprio, Leonardo DiCaprio, Susie Cohen, Marylou Seigel, D. Art Seigel, Larry Kopald, Ronnie Mae Weiss, Daniel Sobol, Jonah Sobol, Betty Bardige, Art Bardige, Ambassador Jimmy Kolker, and Dr. Bob Shillman.

It is good to have friends when traveling alone in Africa, and I am grateful to have had the company of Jackson Komunda, Bucyana Willbroad, Joel Glick, Gershom and Tzippora Sizomu, JJ Keki, Moses Sebagabo, Samson Wamani, Jeffrey Summit, and John Servies. Karen Lotz, Kate Fletcher, and Maryellen Hanley at Candlewick Press have skillfully molded this project together.

• •

First edition 2008

Library of Congress Cataloging-in-Publication Data is available.

Library of Congress Catalog Card Number 2008928356

ISBN 978-0-7636-2281-7

10 9 8 7 6 5 4 3 2 1

Printed in China

This book was typeset in Dante and Interstate.

Candlewick Press
2067 Massachusetts Avenue
Cambridge, Massachusetts 02140

visit us at www.candlewick.com

Breakfast in the Rainforest

» A VISIT WITH MOUNTAIN GORILLAS «

RICHARD SOBOL

with an afterword by **Leonardo DiCaprio**

CANDLEWICK PRESS
CAMBRIDGE, MASSACHUSETTS

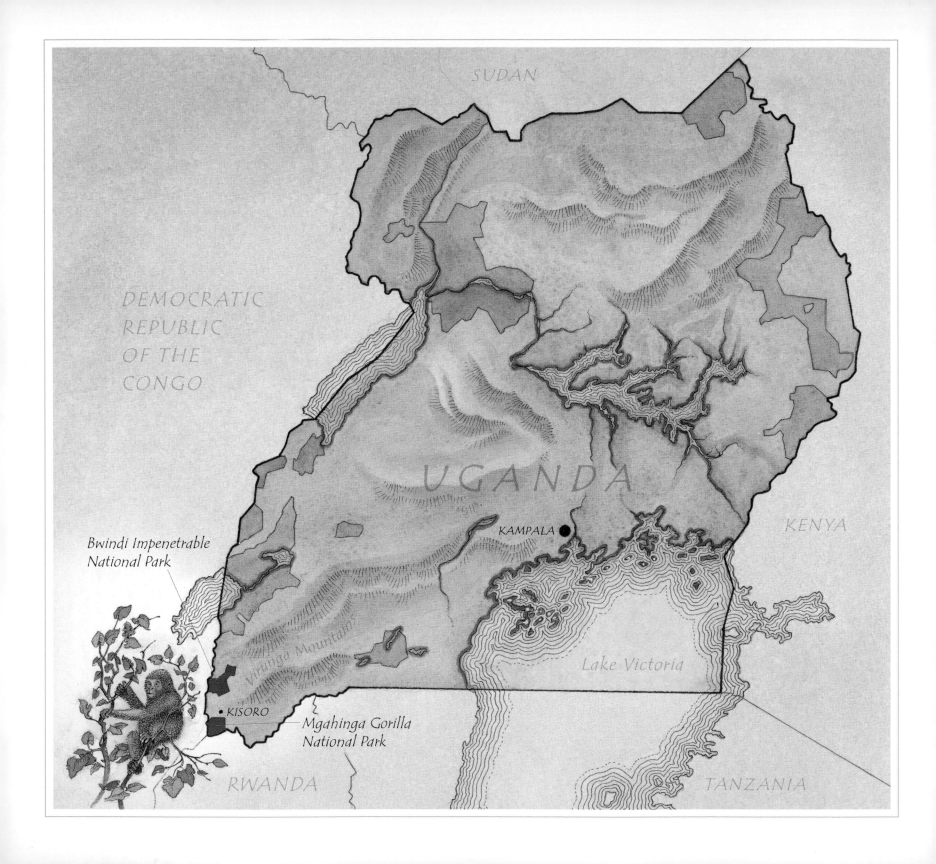

SUDAN

DEMOCRATIC
REPUBLIC
OF THE
CONGO

UGANDA

KENYA

Bwindi Impenetrable
National Park

KAMPALA ●

KISORO

Virunga Mountains

Lake Victoria

Mgahinga Gorilla
National Park

RWANDA

TANZANIA

• •

As a wildlife photographer, I have been chased by a hippo, sprayed by a whale, and licked by an orangutan. With many natural habitats around the world rapidly shrinking and disappearing, I travel the globe to photograph species of endangered animals before they are driven to extinction. One such animal struggling for survival is the mountain gorilla. Unfortunately, there are only about 650 of these powerful yet shy creatures left on earth. Although cartoons and movies often exaggerate gorillas, portraying them as fierce bullies, they are actually quiet, peaceful animals. Fascinated by this contrast, I took the long journey into the lush rainforests of Africa to stare deep into the wide eyes of some of our world's few remaining mountain gorillas. By telling the story of these gorillas and of the people who work to protect them, I hope to share with you a rare experience that few have had, and invite you to join me for breakfast in the rainforest.

Richard Sobol

Getting close enough to photograph some of the few mountain gorillas alive on our planet today is a real challenge. Mountain gorillas don't survive in captivity, so none can be found in zoos. The entire remaining population lives in the dense rainforests of two neighboring national parks in central Africa, nearly seven thousand miles away from my home in New England.

To prepare for my trip, I spent a lot of time researching mountain gorillas. I accumulated a two-foot stack of books on my desk—more than I could ever read! I also talked at length with a gorilla expert at Harvard University and with Farley Mowat, the author who studied and edited the diaries of legendary mountain-gorilla researcher Dian Fossey. All my "homework" helped me to develop a strong scientific knowledge of the lives and habits of mountain gorillas. For instance, I learned that the mountain gorilla is the largest of all primates, the zoological order that includes chimpanzees, orangutans, and even humans. I also learned that mountain gorillas are gentle giants—their strong, muscular chests hide a tender nature. They eat a mostly vegetarian diet, with just a few ants, insects, or termites mixed in to add protein. Searching for food is their full-time job, and most days they are content to swing and climb through the forests, seeking fresh thickets of plants and bushes. Once they find a fertile spot, they stop and munch on leaves and fruits and then take long naps or groom one another. This is the time of day—when the gorillas sit together for breakfast—that I wanted to photograph them.

Once my plane tickets to Uganda have been purchased, it takes me several days to pack all of my gear. There are no camera repair shops in the African backcountry, so I need to check and recheck that everything is working. Cameras, lenses, film, and packs all get tested before I leave. Two Nikon cameras should be enough, but I always take a backup, so I pack three for this journey.

《Houses made from mud, sticks, and grass weave through the countryside of Buhoma, the village closest to the rainforests where I am headed. Throughout the day, wisps of white smoke stream through small holes in the roofs, rising up from the cooking fires burning within.

❯ The gorilla tracking permits I purchase from the Uganda Wildlife Authority cost a small fortune, so I'm glad to know that this money will go toward protecting many of Africa's endangered species.

After two days of flying and a ten-hour wait to change planes in London, I arrive—wobbly and weary—in Kampala, Uganda's capital city. Once there, I pick up my official gorilla tracking permits from the Uganda Wildlife Authority.

There are four gorilla families in Uganda that can be visited by small groups of no more than six people each day. Visitor permits are sometimes reserved more than two years in advance. These permits are expensive: each one-hour session costs more than two hundred dollars—ten times more than a Ugandan National Parks permit for a full day with lions, hippos, or elephants. I pay eight hundred dollars in total for four permits, each to be used on a different day. Money from these permits helps the Uganda Wildlife Authority pay park rangers, buy vehicles, and provide medicine or research studies for other animals that need help. The mountain gorillas are indeed the superstars of all the endangered species in this region, and many other wildlife groups have the gorillas to thank for the resources that keep them safe.

After a day of rest, I hop into a beat-up four-wheel-drive vehicle for the bone-jarring, teeth-rattling, eight-hour ride along the steep, winding mountain roads. We're headed two hundred miles southwest from Kampala to Bwindi Impenetrable National Park. Although the local people call them roads, the hard-packed dirt tracks are more like giant curly fries speckled with big chunks of salt. They weave up in spirals, dotted with piles of rock and dirt that fall from the steep cliffs during the overnight rains. In spite

≫ A boy stops on the side of a bumpy, winding road to repair his blown-out bicycle tire.

of the landscape's sharp angles, the roads are surrounded by fields of bananas, beans, and tea, which hug the sides of the hills. The women and children who plant and work these small gardens ignore the force of gravity, their bare feet pressing into the rich soil so that they can harvest the food that they need for their survival.

≪ Balancing on a steep hillside garden, a woman pauses from tending to her yams and beans to smile for a photograph.

13

❯This boy carries fresh greens for cooking into a Ugandan vegetable stew called *sukumawiki*. His load could weigh as much as twenty pounds.

Because there are few cars or trucks traveling here, the roads become wide sidewalks alive with people, who walk or push bikes along the steep curves. Everyone is carrying something, and often the load is larger than the carrier. Some have huge piles of cut greens; others bring firewood or baskets of vegetables to sell at the market. Many balance containers of water like baseball caps on the top of their heads. Children

have schoolbooks or garden tools with rough wooden handles piled up on the backs of bicycles or homemade scooters. With few spare parts available, most of the bikes are missing pedals or spokes and have rusty chains that clang and squeal as they turn. The scooters are carved out of dried wood and fastened together with pegs and string.

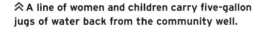

≫ A line of women and children carry five-gallon jugs of water back from the community well.

≫ These boys use scooters they've made themselves to transport water and vegetables.

⩔ **Potatoes for sale on the road to Kisoro. In the background are the Virunga Mountains, extending through three countries — Uganda, Rwanda, and the Democratic Republic of the Congo.**

As I near Kisoro, the town closest to where the mountain gorillas live, one set of jagged peaks replaces another around each winding corner, and the long rays of sunlight fall into deep shadows. In this small corner of Africa, Uganda, Rwanda, and the Democratic Republic of the Congo meet in a chain of rough mountains called the Virungas. The steep slopes all around me are part of an active volcanic range that thrusts high up into the soft rain clouds. It is here that the last remaining mountain gorillas make their home, divided almost equally between two areas that are protected and monitored by National Park rangers. The two populations once lived together in a single large forest.

Little by little, over hundreds of years, African farmers cleared land in the central valley of the gorilla habitat, and the gorillas slowly divided into separate groups, one half living along the Virunga volcanoes and the other half in Bwindi Impenetrable National Park. Although they now live only thirty miles apart, these two populations of gorillas will never meet or even know that each other exists.

Both groups, however, are affected by common problems. During the thirty-five-year life span of these gorillas, the three neighboring countries have all experienced violent civil wars. At different times over the past two decades, the gorillas have heard blasts of gunfire on all sides of their habitats. At other times poachers have made war on the helpless gorillas themselves. These battles, combined with the farming needs of the ever-expanding human population nearby, have shrunk the home range of the mountain gorillas so that it can barely sustain them.

During my visit to Uganda, I am planning to see both the population in Bwindi and the one in the Virungas, in a national park called Mgahinga. To coordinate visitors, the Uganda Wildlife Authority has an office on the dusty main street of Kisoro that is wedged between an open-air barbershop and a pharmacy called the Human Drug Shop. I check in and meet thirty-two-year-old Silver Mbonigaba (em-bo-nee-GAH-bah), who will be my guide on this expedition. Lean and muscular, with a broad smile, Silver grew up on the border of Bwindi Impenetrable National Park and always dreamed of working as a park ranger. As we sit and share a bottle

⌃ A sign outside a grocery store in Kisoro shows the pride local people feel toward the gorillas.

« The drugstore next to the Wildlife Authority office. *Who else but humans might shop there?* I wonder.

⌃ Silver Mbonigaba, the chief ranger of Bwindi Impenetrable National Park, uses a two-way radio to talk with other rangers inside the park.

of neon-red, super-sugary Ugandan soda, he explains some of the local history to me.

When Silver was a small boy, Bwindi was called the "Impenetrable Forest"—a wildlife-filled place that few people dared enter. Not until twenty years ago, after the discovery of almost three hundred mountain gorillas living within this dense forest, did scientists who had been working nearby in the Virungas come here to study them. Naturally shy and fearful, the gorillas stayed hidden in the trees. At first, researchers rarely saw a gorilla and learned what they could from the nests and droppings that the gorillas left behind as they traveled through the tightly woven forest. As they slowly gained the gorillas' acceptance, the researchers learned that mountain gorillas live together in small family troops led by the largest male. This leader is called a silverback because of the dramatic wedge of light fur that covers his back. The adult gorillas consume between forty and fifty pounds of food each day. Since the leaves, shoots, bark, insects and berries that they eat are small and lightweight, gorillas spend almost half of each day looking for food.

I listen closely to Silver, but it is clear that an announcement has been broadcast to all the local mosquitoes—fresh blood has arrived in town. My hands, neck, and ankles are soon dotted with bites. "They seem to know when a *mzungu* arrives," he says with a laugh as he grabs a bottle of repellent for me. "*Mzungu* is our word for European and white visitors," he explains. Soon, I stink of DEET, having sprayed myself with enough slime to keep both mosquitoes and all other animals away, and Silver continues to tell me all he knows about the gorillas.

Gorillas have strong bonds with one another and stay close together in family troops of ten to twenty. The males and females both care for and play with their young. This is most obvious during the late mornings after they have eaten, when they find a comfy place to nap during the heat of midday. The babies and smaller gorillas cling to the adults as family members groom one

≫ A home and farm on the edge of the "Impenetrable Forest," which is one of the richest unexplored ecosystems in Africa.

⌄ Rangers begin a patrol in Mgahinga National Park at the base of the Virunga Mountains.

another—picking bugs and gunk out of their deep fur. The babies will nurse and cling tightly to their mothers for their first six months. During this time, they see and smell the foods that their mothers are eating, and are often showered with the crumbs and splinters that are the gorilla version of processed baby food. Mom will also teach her baby which foods not to eat by grabbing away the many poisonous plants that could make it sick. This is how the babies learn to recognize approximately sixty plants and trees that will make up their diet as they grow older and more independent. A baby gorilla will venture farther away from its mother's grasp—little by little—until it is about three years old and finally on its own.

I rise the next morning before daybreak and drive from Kisoro to my first rendezvous with the gorillas. The dense forest that defines the border of the protected conservation land of Bwindi Impenetrable National Park is easy to find. Orderly patches of potatoes and bananas grow right up to its rough edges. In addition to its 350 mountain gorillas, this rich rainforest is home to an abundance of wildlife. It holds more than 100 different mammals, 350 types of birds, 400 different butterflies, and more than 200 kinds of trees. All of this is in an area that is only one-tenth the size of greater Boston, where I live.

Silver Mbonigaba is now the chief ranger here at Bwindi, having spent every day of the last four years in the company of gorillas. At first the gorillas would flee deep into the forest when he and his trackers approached, but over time, the gorillas grew comfortable with the rangers, allowing them to get closer and closer. At sunrise each morning, Silver leaves the small house that he shares with his family and treks to meet the gorillas. These daily early-morning ranger visits help to preserve the gorillas' acceptance of humans. As the morning continues, small groups of tourists accompany the trackers. The tourists' hotel and guide fees help support the local people, as well as the community's schools and medical clinics. Tips for service help the guides build homes for their families, expand their gardens, and perhaps even buy livestock that will help feed their families.

⌃ Silver tends to his small herd of goats, which provide fresh milk and cheese for his family.

❯❯ Schoolchildren living on the edge of Bwindi Impenetrable National Park take special pride in their gorilla neighbors. As I approached, they cheered and shouted, "Hello, *mzungu*. How are you, *mzungu?*"

At the edge of the forest, Silver explains that there are many strict rules that all visitors must follow. First and foremost, he tells me that when we see the gorillas, we cannot disturb them. He firmly explains that my visit will be limited to exactly one hour; any longer might alter the gorillas' regular daily patterns. No eating, no flash photography, no talking, no getting closer than fifteen feet, and last of all, no sneezing—since sneezing could send germs through the air and make the gorillas sick.

The family of gorillas that I will visit first is called the Nkuringo (en-koo-RING-go) group. They are named for the little village next to where they were first seen. Although Silver and his team have been tracking these gorillas for four years, I will be the first photographer and pale-skinned visitor that the Nkuringo gorillas have encountered. I look so different from Silver and his team, with their dark African skin. I ask Silver what the Nkuringo gorillas will think of my pale complexion. "Don't worry," he assures me with a laugh. "With all of those cameras, the gorillas will hardly notice your skin color!"

As we pass a few mud huts and banana fields on the edge of the park, the terraced gardens of the local farmers give way to the sharp line of uncut forest. People live right up to the boundary of Bwindi, and the gorillas do not always understand that they cannot eat the farmers' crops. Locals were surprised to learn that they are the only people — in Africa or the rest of the world — who live next to mountain gorillas. This

≫ A hut made of leaves, sticks, and mud is nestled on the edge of Bwindi Impenetrable National Park.

makes them proud of their special role in helping to keep watch over their famous neighbors. If the gorillas stray from the park, the villagers alert Silver and his team, who chase them back across the borderline and into the safety of the forest.

Mountain gorillas can spend almost all morning sitting and eating. Once the gorillas find a natural cafeteria of leaves, green bamboo, or wild celery roots to stop at for breakfast, they settle in and take their time feasting. Since this is when Silver and his team of rangers usually check in on them, the Nkuringo gorillas have gotten used to people visiting them during breakfast.

⌃ Park rangers check and note their position deep within the forest.

Crossing into the park this early morning, we quickly begin our steep climb to visit the gorillas. There are no paths, sidewalks, or chairlifts for human guests. Once I plunge into the thick, wet forest, I have to overcome the same obstacles that the gorillas contend with each day.

Silver opens his frayed notebook and checks the last location where the Nkuringo gorillas were observed yesterday. This will become the starting point for today's trek. As we move through the walls of brush, the trackers look for signs. Broken branches, piles of dung, and tracks in the mud offer clues to finding the path that the gorillas have made in their search for fresh food.

I struggle and slip with each step on the wet roots and mud. The brown earth has been transformed into a slippery mush, and I feel like I am trying to catch my grip on a semifrozen waterfall. I grasp for branches and vines to

≫ This rapid stream is one of many obstacles we encounter as we follow the gorillas. You can see why a walking stick comes in very handy in the jungle!

pull myself up, using muscles that I never knew I had. I feel as if I, too, am becoming an ape, crawling over fallen logs through dense brush and vines that seem determined to capture and strangle me as I try to pass.

The lead tracker finds our first clue that gorillas are close: a wide, flat pile of spongy leaves and branches. These are the nests the gorillas slept in the night before. The forest flies have already found this fresh dung inside the nests and sent out word that breakfast was served. Thousands and thousands of buzzing specks swarm around, creating dark living clouds that feast on the gorilla droppings. As I look for a clear spot to stop and take a picture, I hear branches snapping and realize it is the gorillas racing up the hillside, searching for a breakfast buffet of their own.

Following Silver, I crawl ahead. Long vines with sharp thorns attack my fingers as I move forward. I brush against a thick bush, and its stinging flowers grab on to my wet shirt and stick pointed needles into my shoulders. With my upper body under attack from the vegetation, I look down at a parade of red fire ants as they climb over my boots to

⩔ Silver points out fresh dung in an overnight nest — our first sign that the gorillas are nearby!

△ Silver leads a team of rangers through the brush. He uses his sharp machete, known as a *panga*, to clear a trail through the dense rainforest.

bite and sting my legs. Now I don't know where to scratch or rub; little pains are everywhere!

"Come on," Silver urges me. "We're almost with them now." Swinging his machete, he quickly cuts through the brush and heavy vines to clear a three-foot-wide tunnel for me to peer through. Stopping and smiling widely, he whispers, "Now look through these branches; the gorillas are here. They have stopped to eat and we have found them."

I am pulled in two directions: should I grab my camera, or should I simply look ahead to see — with my own eyes — the mountain gorillas whom I have traveled so far to meet? I remind myself that I am here as a photographer and that my first glimpse should come to me through a lens.

I try to balance both of my cameras: one loaded with extra-sensitive film for the deep shadows of the forest floor and a second with slower film for the strong sunlight higher up in the trees. Sweat pours down my face and drips onto the cameras as I strain for my first view of a mountain gorilla. I am totally drenched from the heat and the hike. My body is leaking like one of those watering hoses covered with spray holes. Silver moves toward me and pulls a dry handkerchief out of his coat pocket. He leans in and says, "Here, take this to dry off your lenses." Winking at me, he adds, "Now you know why it's called a rainforest."

Through the brush I can hear the crunching of leaves and snapping of twigs, breaking the silence like popcorn being munched in a quiet movie theater. The smell is strong, too—like nothing I have ever experienced before. It is rising from caked bits of poop, sweat, food crumbs, and jungle junk that has stuck together and baked into clinging knots in the gorillas' hair. At first I see a patch of black hair. It could be a shoulder, or maybe it's a knee.

I look through my camera again and see a pair of deep, wide eyes shining bright red, like ripe cherries. I press the shutter; I have found the moment that I came here to photograph.

» » »

A vine moves, and I see a row of wide, knobby fingers place a bouquet of spiny-tipped leaves into a round bulb of a mouth. My finger presses the camera's shutter button, and I record my first mountain gorilla, a female who is carefully selecting the sweetest branches to munch on. As she raises her thick arms for more, she looks as if she is moving in slow motion.

When the silverback settles in to slowly chew on some leaves, I gently edge myself a few feet closer.
The wall of plants opens up just enough to create a soft green frame around him.

Higher up in the treetops, the sunlight shines brightly on the thick, dark coats of the gorillas. With all that light, it is easier for me to spot them and to focus my camera on them, even as they swing among the branches.

This moment, frozen on film, transports
me back in time to the ancient forest
where humankind was born. These
gorillas are our close biological cousins,
and so their home was our home
long before roads and houses were built.

A one-year-old gorilla emerges from the branches for a few seconds. I have just enough time to focus and hold down the shutter button to get this sequence of photographs.

This mother gorilla keeps a close watch on her baby. The baby will nurse for about a year before gradually adding other foods to its diet.

The gorilla's home on the
dewy-wet forest floor is filled with vines, bushes, and stalks. I play a kind of peekaboo,
moving an inch or two — up, down, or to the side — in order to get this gorilla's face clearly in my frame.

Sixty minutes race by. I am surprised when Silver taps on his watch and holds up two fingers, signaling that we are nearing the end of our visit. It seems as if we only just arrived. My eye stays glued to my camera, hoping for one more picture. Silver tugs on my sleeve. "We must leave them now and give them back the forest."

Reluctantly, I turn away, my pockets bursting with used film cans. We hike back through the same challenging terrain, but this time with a sense of calm. The urgency of the morning has passed. I have met the Nkuringo gorillas and will return to photograph them again tomorrow and the next day. Then I will leave Bwindi to spend a day with the mountain gorillas down the road in Mgahinga National Park.

Although I am in Uganda, an English-speaking country in central Africa, the plight of the mountain gorilla repeats itself in neighboring Rwanda and the Democratic Republic of the Congo (formerly known as Zaire). The problems facing the mountain gorillas, and the benefits that tourism brings to the local people and the animals, are shared in all three countries.

« The view toward Kisoro as we hike out of the rainforest in the late afternoon.

But the gorillas themselves have no passports. They travel internationally, without visas or tour guides, as they pursue food supplies on all sides of the border that cuts into their small home range. When gorillas from Mgahinga National Park in Uganda cross over into Rwanda during

⌃ An adult male, or "silverback," leads the Nkuringo group through the forest. A full-grown silverback can weigh more than four hundred pounds and is the largest of all primates.

the dry season, the park rangers of both countries work together to ensure the safety of the animals. The Ugandan rangers track the troop right up to the edge of the park and radio the location to the Rwandan rangers, who wait to meet them on the other side. The gorillas are thus ambassadors, bringing people together.

Once out of the forest, I collapse from exhaustion. In the late afternoon, I sit by the fireplace at the Travellers Rest Hotel in Kisoro, my muscles stretched and sore from the morning's long, steep climb deep into the "impenetrable" depths of Bwindi. My body aches, and I am happy to be inside and resting. A loud thunderclap jerks me up and out of my cozy chair. Following the explosion, pounding rain smacks against the thin roof of my sitting room. A trickle of water falls from the small gaps in the grass roof and splashes onto my arm. Searching for something to dry myself with, I reach into my pocket and pull out a handkerchief. It is the one that Silver gave me this morning in the damp forest—his gift to me. I arrived in Africa hoping to encounter a silverback, and now I also have a new friend named Silver.

≪ My new friend, Silver Mbonigaba, with his family

As I look outside, my gaze follows the rushing streams that carry away gobs of dust and brown dirt in long tangles that look like chocolate milk moving through a drinking straw. I stare into the gray mist that covers the outlines of the mountains and the forests. I am within twenty miles of all of the mountain gorillas in the world, and the entire

⌃ Rain clouds move in over the gorilla homes in the Virunga Mountains in Uganda, Rwanda, and the Democratic Republic of the Congo.

species is sharing this downpour with me. Rain is now falling in all three countries that are home to the gorillas. Every known mountain gorilla is getting wet now, his or her dark coat soaking up water like a thick black sponge. As I listen to the clattering of the rainfall, I wonder if there is any other place on earth where the survival of a single species is linked together in an area the size of a lone storm cloud.

Even though I wasn't invited to sit down and join in the feast, I am grateful to have observed a breakfast in the rainforest. And, unlike the gorillas, I am not a vegetarian, and am eager to try whatever the chef puts out on the table tonight—if only I can stay awake long enough for dinner. . . .

>> This is the photograph I dreamed of taking on my journey to East Africa: the gentle touch of a powerful mountain gorilla nibbling on a single leaf during breakfast.

Mountain Gorilla Facts

Scientific name *Gorilla beringei beringei*

Home range central Africa

Population 650–700 living in the wild, zero in captivity

Average adult weight female: 200–250 pounds; male: 450–500 pounds

Diet primarily vegetarian. Gorillas eat more than one hundred different types of leaves, flowers, fruit, and fungus, as well as a few insects. They do not drink any additional water; they get all the liquid they need from the large amounts of plant life that they consume.

Average life span 35 years

Reproduction Females first give birth at around ten years old and then continue to have a baby every three or four years.

Social structure Closely knit groups of 10–20 members live and move together.

Conservation status critically endangered. Mountain gorillas are among the most threatened of all the primate species.

• •

Websites for More Information

African Wildlife Foundation • www.awf.org

The Dian Fossey Gorilla Fund International • www.gorillafund.org

The Gorilla Organization • www.gorillas.org

International Gorilla Conservation Programme • www.igcp.org

Leonardo DiCaprio's Eco-Site • www.leonardodicaprio.org

The Uganda Wildlife Authority • www.uwa.or.ug

The Uganda Wildlife Education Centre • www.uweczoo.org

Glossary

Bwindi Impenetrable National Park the newest of Uganda's protected national parks. This is home to half of the world's mountain gorillas.

endangered species groups of animals or plants whose populations are so diminished that they are in danger of becoming extinct

film a light-sensitive material used for recording a photographic image

focus the clarity or sharpness of a photographic image

frame the boundaries of a camera's viewfinder

habitat natural area that is home to an animal or plant

Kampala the capital city of Uganda

Kisoro Ugandan town on the border with Rwanda and close to Mgahinga and Bwindi Impenetrable National Parks

Mgahinga Gorilla National Park Ugandan national park on the border with Rwanda and the Democratic Republic of the Congo

mzungu (mah-ZOONG-goo) the term for a white man or white woman in Swahili and many Bantu languages in East Africa

Nkuringo village on the border of Bwindi Impenetrable National Park; also the name of the gorilla group that lives there

panga a sharp, long blade used to cut trails in the jungle

poacher someone who illegally hunts wildlife

primate the group of mammals that includes humans, monkeys, and apes

rainforest a wet, evergreen, tropical forest

shutter the window that opens and closes to let light pass through a camera lens onto a piece of film or a digital imaging sensor

silverback a mature male mountain gorilla

sukumawiki (soo-koo-mah-WEE-kee) Ugandan vegetable stew

Virungas the volcanic mountain range in central Africa that is home to the mountain gorillas in Uganda, Rwanda, and the Democratic Republic of the Congo

Afterword
Leonardo DiCaprio

For ages, gorillas have fascinated us, perhaps because they are very much like us, with more than 95 percent of their DNA identical to ours. Gorillas are the largest of the primates and live in the beautiful forested mountains of central Africa. Sadly, today, mountain gorillas are threatened by extinction due to human activities. There are only 650 of these remarkable creatures left in the world. What a tragedy it would be to lose these creatures that are so close to us.

Gorillas are at risk for various reasons; they are losing their lives due to poaching, loss of habitat, war, and disease. Human communities are encroaching on the gorillas' mountain home and because of that, they catch human diseases; gorillas are no longer hidden, so they are vulnerable to poaching; and war rages in the gorilla mountain region, further accelerating their decline.

Raising public awareness around the pressing issues of environmental degradation, climate change, and species extinction is an essential first step to conserving endangered species and ecosystems. Richard Sobol has traveled around the world for wildlife conservation. His book *Breakfast in the Rainforest: A Visit with Mountain Gorillas* gives young children the opportunity to fall in love with gorillas and to better understand them. With this book, children can discover how important the survival of the gorillas is and how they can make a difference in the world.

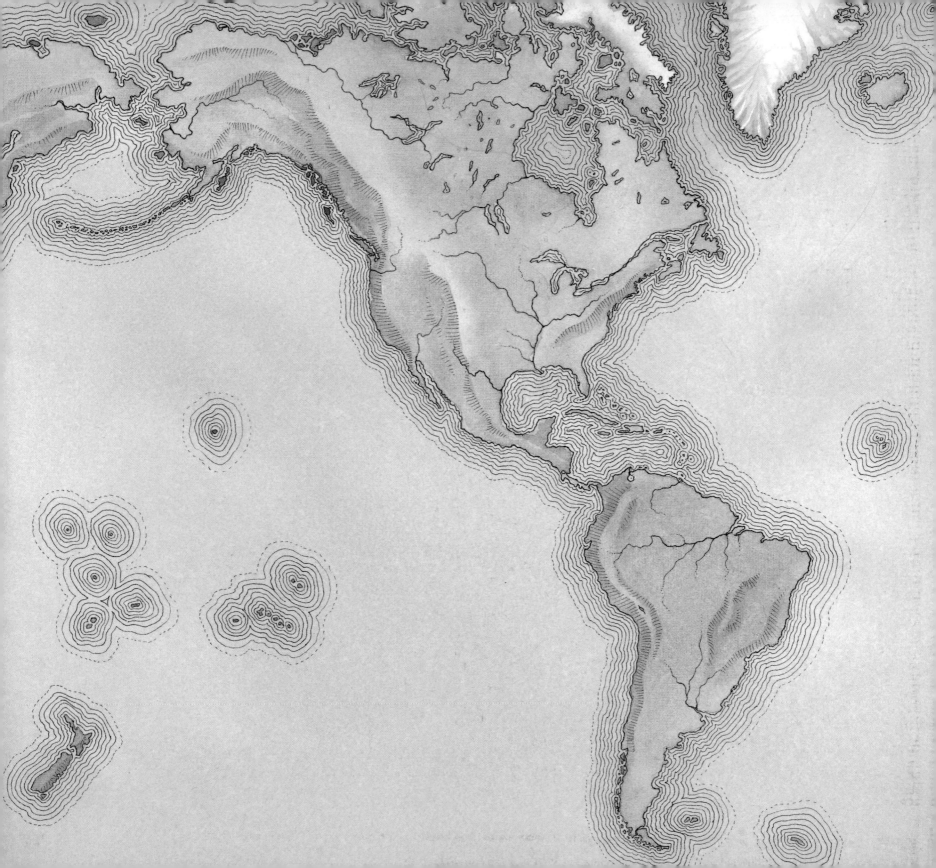